T0379087

WEATHER AND SEASON FACTS

by
William Anthony

BEARPORT
PUBLISHING

Minneapolis, Minnesota

Library of Congress Cataloging-in-Publication Data

Names: Anthony, William, 1996– author.
Title: Weather and season facts / by William Anthony.
Description: Fusion books. | Minneapolis, Minnesota : Bearport Publishing Company, [2022] | Series: Fact-o-graphics! | Includes bibliographical references and index.
Identifiers: LCCN 2021005276 (print) | LCCN 2021005277 (ebook) | ISBN 9781647479909 (library binding) | ISBN 9781647479954 (paperback) | ISBN 9781636910000 (ebook)
Subjects: LCSH: Weather—Juvenile literature. | Seasons—Juvenile literature.
Classification: LCC QC981.3 .H335 2022 (print) | LCC QC981.3 (ebook) | DDC 551.6—dc23
LC record available at https://lccn.loc.gov/2021005276
LC ebook record available at https://lccn.loc.gov/2021005277

For more information, write to Bearport Publishing, 5357 Penn Avenue South, Minneapolis, MN 55419. Printed in the United States of America.

Photo credits:
5 - Ryerson Clark, Dmitry Rukhlenko, Regina F. Silva, curiosity, uiliaaa, Martial Red, aShatilov, 8 - Artsem Vysotski, 9 - Melvin Sandelin, vladsilver, JIMMOYHT, Amanita Silvicora, 10 - Boyloso, avian, 11 - Dmitry Naumov, 12 - avian, 13 - Dario Lo Presti, 14 - Nattapol_Sritongcom, intararit, 15 - gdagys, 16 - YanLev, Katerina Pereverzeva, 17 - CreativeAngela, 18 - Den Rozhnovsky, Graphics RF, 19 - NotionPic, Sunny_nsk, 20 - Valeri Hadeev, Renee's illustrations, Alexey Seafarer, Ondrej Prosicky, 21 - Sergey Uryadnikov, fmajor, BigMouse, matrioshka, Tarikdiz, 22 - Justin Hobson, BreezyVector, Rvector, Vectors Bang, 23 - Sunny Forest, MSSA, Javid Kheyrabadi, Maike Hildebrandt.

Images are courtesy of Shutterstock.com. With thanks to Getty Images, Thinkstock Photo and iStockphoto.

CONTENTS

Weather 4

Seasons 6

Temperature 8

Sunshine 10

Clouds and Wind 12

Rain and Floods 14

Snow 16

Thunder and Lightning 18

Animals and Weather 20

Extreme Weather 22

Glossary 24

Index 24

WEATHER

Weather is what you can see in the sky and feel in the air outside. There are lots of types of weather.

Sunny and warm

Rainy and cloudy

Snowy and cold

Weather is what's going on outside right now.

Windy

4

Humans live in places with all kinds of weather. Some places can be very cold and snowy. Others are very hot and sunny.

Different foods grow better in different types of weather.

Bananas grow best in hot weather.

Spinach grows best in cold weather.

5

SEASONS

The seasons are the four times of the year. In most parts of the world, each season has different weather. Summer is usually the hottest season, and winter is the coldest season.

Spring

Summer

Fall

Winter

The seasons are opposite in the top and bottom halves of the globe. So when it's spring in North America, it's fall in South America!

Earth is **tilted** as it moves around the sun. At different times of the year, Earth tilts to and away from the sun. Summer is when we tilt to the sun. Winter is when we tilt away.

Winter starts on December 21st in North America.

The exact same day is the beginning of summer in Australia.

TEMPERATURE

Temperature is how hot or cold something is. Different seasons have different temperatures.

In some places, winter can be cold and snowy. Summer can be hot and sunny. Fall and spring are in between, with some rainy days.

Water **freezes** at 32 degrees Fahrenheit (0 degrees Celsius). Lakes can freeze in very cold winters.

8

The hottest place on Earth is Death Valley in California. The summer temperature is about 117°F (47°C).

The coldest place on Earth is Antarctica. The temperature can drop to about -148°F (-100°C). *Brrr!*

SUNSHINE

Earth spins as it moves around the sun. Day is when our part of Earth is facing the sun. Night is when we are facing away from it. Days are shorter in the winter and longer in the summer.

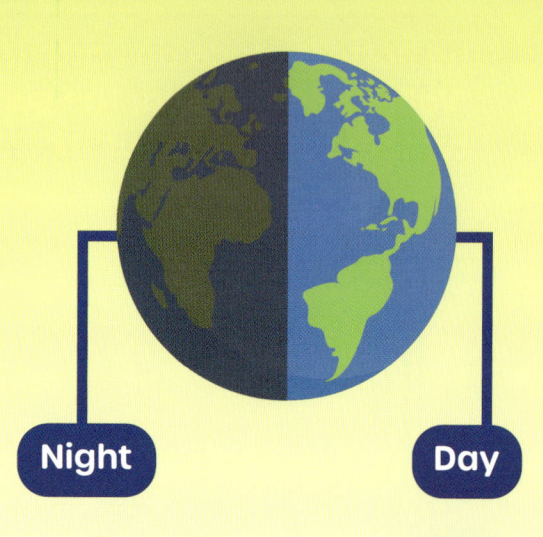

Night   Day

The city of Reykjavik in Iceland has the longest day of the year. On the first day of summer, it gets more than 21 hours of daylight!

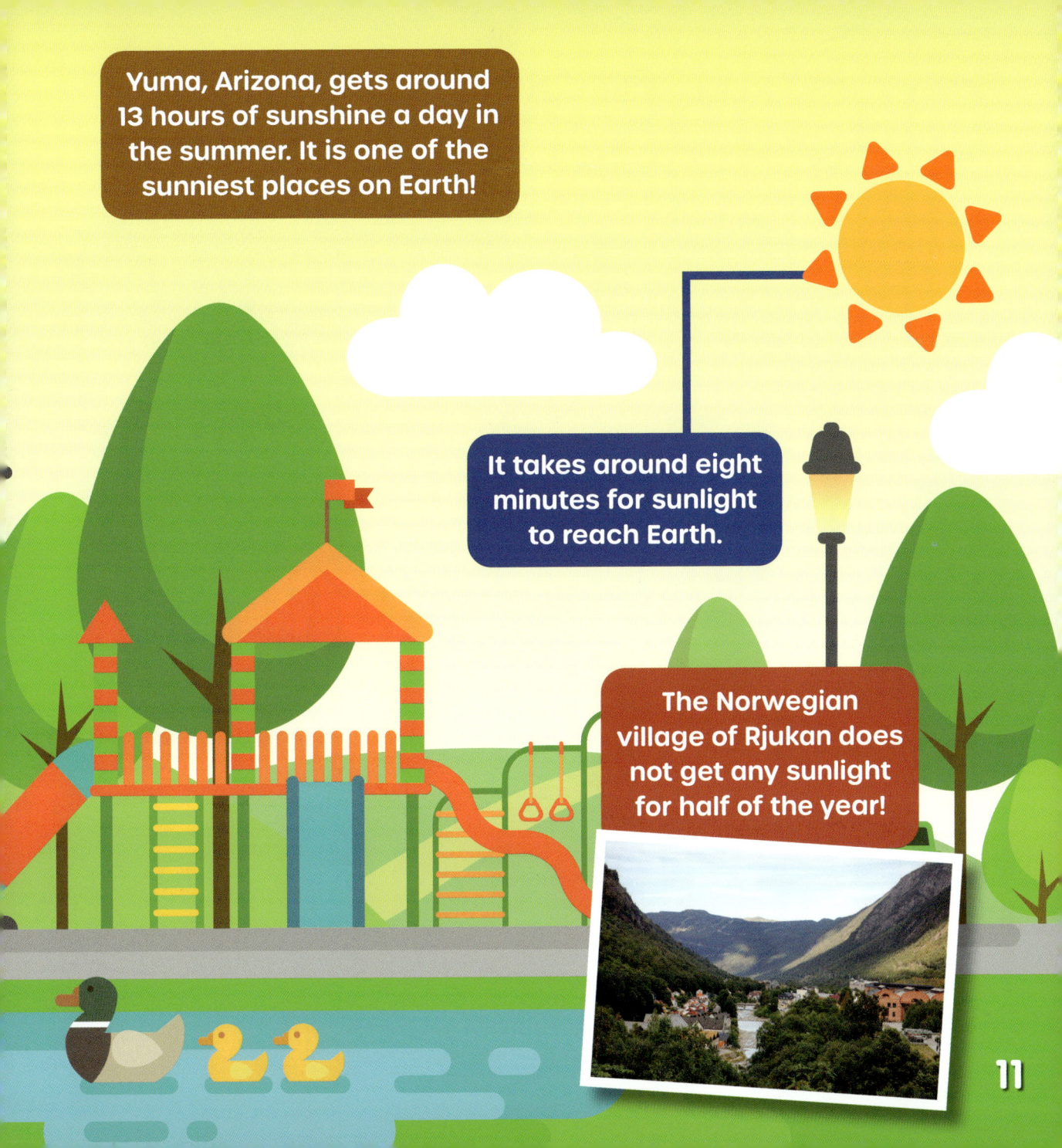

Yuma, Arizona, gets around 13 hours of sunshine a day in the summer. It is one of the sunniest places on Earth!

It takes around eight minutes for sunlight to reach Earth.

The Norwegian village of Rjukan does not get any sunlight for half of the year!

CLOUDS AND WIND

Clouds float high in the sky. They are made when warm air on the ground rises into the sky and gets colder. The warm air has tiny drops of water in it. As the air rises, the water comes together into clouds.

When the warm air rises, colder air rushes in to take its place. This rushing air is wind.

12

Very tall clouds often bring strong thunderstorms.

Some clouds can look big, white, and fluffy. They usually mean good weather.

Low, flat, gray clouds that cover most of the sky usually bring rain.

Fog is a type of cloud that is found very close to the ground.

RAIN AND FLOODS

When the water in clouds becomes too heavy, it falls from the sky as rain.

Raindrops can fall as fast as 18 miles per hour (29 kmp).

We need rain to give us drinking water. Plants and trees need water, too.

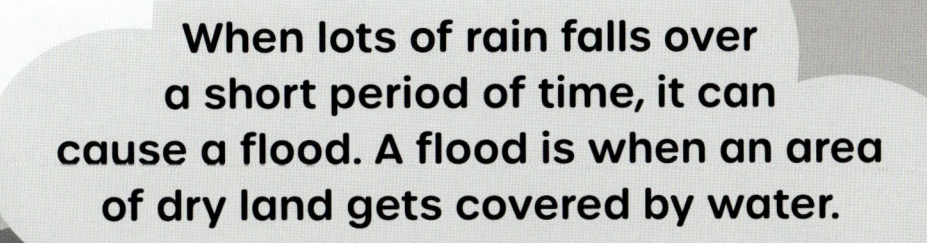

When lots of rain falls over a short period of time, it can cause a flood. A flood is when an area of dry land gets covered by water.

The rainiest place on Earth is the Indian village of Mawsynram. It gets about 467 inches (1,186 cm) of rain a year!

Floods can be very unsafe. The water can fill up cars and homes.

15

SNOW

Some water in clouds turns to ice. When it gets heavy, it falls from the clouds. Then, the ice clumps together to form snow!

No two snowflakes look the same, but most have six sides.

The best snow for making snowballs and snow people has more water in it. The water makes the snowflakes stick together better.

16

When falling snow is mixed with strong winds, it is called a blizzard.

The Japanese city of Aomori is the snowiest place on Earth. It gets about 312 in. (792 cm) of snow a year!

Light and fluffy snow is called powder.

Snow melts when it gets above 32°F (0°C).

THUNDER AND LIGHTNING

A thunderstorm is a type of weather known for its dark clouds, flashes of light, and booming sounds. The flashes are called lightning, and the sounds are called thunder.

Thunderstorms happen when hot, wet air rises quickly and hits colder air. As the warm air cools, clouds and rain form.

Electricity in rain clouds creates lightning. The heat in lightning leads to the sound of thunder.

We see lightning before we hear thunder. This is because light travels faster than sound.

The sound of thunder travels around 10 times faster than a cheetah.

Thunderstorms are usually around 15 miles (24 km) wide.

ANIMALS AND WEATHER

Animals have **adapted** to the weather where they live.

Meerkats have dark circles around their eyes that act like sunglasses. They live in bright and sunny Africa, so this helps them to see.

An arctic fox changes the color of its fur with the seasons. In the winter, it has white fur that blends in with the snow. But in the summer, its fur is gray or brown to match the rest of its home.

Polar bears live in the freezing cold Arctic. They have thick fur to keep them warm.

Kangaroos lick their arms to stay cool in the dry Australian heat.

EXTREME WEATHER

Weather can get extreme! Extreme weather can be strange, surprising, and very powerful.

Sometimes, chunks of ice fall from clouds during storms. This is called hail. The largest piece of hail ever found was almost the size of a volleyball!

Winds in the strongest **tornadoes** can spin at more than 185 miles per hour (298 kph).

Droughts are long periods of time with no rain. They can cause plants to die.

Thundersnow is a thunderstorm where snow falls instead of rain. There can even be snow lightning!

In very dry places, strong winds can pick up dirt, dust, and sand. They create dust storms that can rise over 20,000 feet (6,096 m) into the sky!

GLOSSARY

adapted changed over time in order to face new settings and challenges

electricity a kind of energy that makes heat and light

extreme far beyond what is usual or expected

freezes gets so cold that it turns solid, such as water turning into ice

tilted leaning to the side

tornadoes storms with very strong winds that swirl in a cone shape

INDEX

clouds 4, 12–14, 16, 18, 22

cold 4–6, 8–9, 12, 18, 21

Earth 7, 9–11, 15, 17

food 5

hot 5–6, 8–9, 18

humans 5

light 10–11, 18–19

sound 18–19

sun 4–5, 7, 10–11, 20

water 8, 12, 14–16